Rockhopper Penguin

by Jessica Rudolph

Consultant: Thane Maynard, Director
Cincinnati Zoo and Botanical Garden
Cincinnati, Ohio

BEARPORT PUBLISHING

New York, New York

Credits

Cover, © sunsinger/Shutterstock; TOC, © sunsinger/Shutterstock; 4–5, © Linda More/Fotolia; 6T, © Volt Collection/Shutterstock; 6M, © MichaelStubblefield/iStock; 6B, © Stubblefield Photography/Shutterstock; 7, © Cheryl Schneider/Alamy; 8, © kirza/iStock; 9, © sunsinger/Shutterstock; 10–11, © imageBROKER/Alamy; 12T, © panda3800/Shutterstock; 12B, © Chris Howey/Shutterstock; 14–15, © marina durante/Shutterstock; 15T, © Evgeny Kovalev spb/Shutterstock; 16–17, © Steve Allen/Shutterstock; 18–19, © Andy Rouse/Photoshot; 20L, © Giedriius/Shutterstock; 20R, © NICOLAS LARENTO/Fotolia; 21, © Fredy Thuerig/Shutterstock; 22T, © webguzs/iStock; 22M, © National Geographic Image Collection/Alamy; 22B, © feathercollector/Shutterstock; 23TL, © Steve Allen/Shutterstock; 23TR, © FannyOldfield/iStock; 23BL, © holbox/Shutterstock; 23BR, © MagMac83/Shutterstock.

Publisher: Kenn Goin
Editor: J. Clark
Creative Director: Spencer Brinker
Design: Debrah Kaiser
Photo Researcher: Olympia Shannon

Library of Congress Cataloging-in-Publication Data

Rudolph, Jessica, author.
  Rockhopper penguin / by Jessica Rudolph.
     pages cm. — (Weird But cute)
  Includes bibliographical references and index.
  ISBN 978-1-62724-848-8 (library binding) — ISBN 1-62724-848-X (library binding)
  1. Eudyptes chrysocome—Juvenile literature. 2. Crested penguins—Juvenile literature. [1. Penguins.] I. Title.
  QL696.S473R83 2016
  598.47—dc23
                                        2015008812

For more information, write to Bearport Publishing Company, Inc., 45 West 21st Street, Suite 3B, New York, New York 10010. Printed in the United States of America.

10 9 8 7 6 5 4 3 2 1

Contents

What's this weird but cute animal?

Spiky, yellow feathers!

It's a **rockhopper penguin.**

Red **eye**s! Orange beak!

5

Hop. Hop. Hop.

Rockhopper
penguins hop
around **steep** rocks.

That's how they got their name.

Rockhoppers spend lots of time in the ocean and on rocky islands.

Rockhoppers are
a kind of bird.

They're about 2 feet
(61 cm) tall.

golden
retriever

Rockhoppers are
as tall as golden
retrievers.

Penguins can't fly.

They are great swimmers, though!

wing

Penguins use their wings like **flippers** to push them through the water.

Rockhoppers look for food in the ocean.

They gobble up squids, crabs, and small fish.

squid

crab

These birds can dive more than 300 feet (91 m) under the water.

Watch out!

Sharks hunt penguins
in the ocean.

skua

blue shark

Birds such as skuas
(SKYOO-uhz) hunt
for penguin eggs
and chicks on land.

15

Rockhoppers live in large groups called **colonies**.

A colony may have 100,000 penguins!

Penguins can trumpet, squeal, and bark. This is how they talk to each other.

penguin colony

17

Fur seals and rockhoppers live on the same islands.

The seals rest on the **shore**.

The penguins hop around them.

Like penguins, fur seals spend time in the water and on land.

18

fur seal

Rockhoppers hatch from eggs.

egg

chick

Chicks don't have spiky yellow feathers.

However, one day they'll look just like their parents!

Both the mother and father penguins take care of their babies.

21

More Weird Birds

Hoatzin
The hoatzin (waht-SEEN) has spiky head feathers. The bird is also known as the stinkbird. The leaves it eats cause the bird to smell like cow poop!

Rhinoceros Hornbill
This bird has a body part on top of its beak called a casque. The casque looks like a rhino's horn. It helps the bird's calls travel for long distances.

Wilson's Bird-of-Paradise
The male Wilson's bird-of-paradise has curly tail feathers and brightly colored wings. It also has a patch of bare skin on its head that's blue.

Glossary

colonies (KOL-uh-neez) groups of animals that live together

flippers (FLIP-urz) body parts that some sea animals such as dolphins use to help them swim

shore (SHOR) the land along the edge of a lake, river, or ocean

steep (STEEP) having a sharp slope or slant

Index

Read More

Owen, Ruth. *Penguin Chicks (Water Babies).* New York: Bearport (2013).

Pringle, Laurence. *Penguins! Strange and Wonderful.* Honesdale, PA: Boyds Mills (2007).

Learn More Online

To learn more about rockhopper penguins, visit **www.bearportpublishing.com/WeirdButCute**

About the Author

Jessica Rudolph lives in Connecticut. She has edited and written many books about history, science, and nature for children.